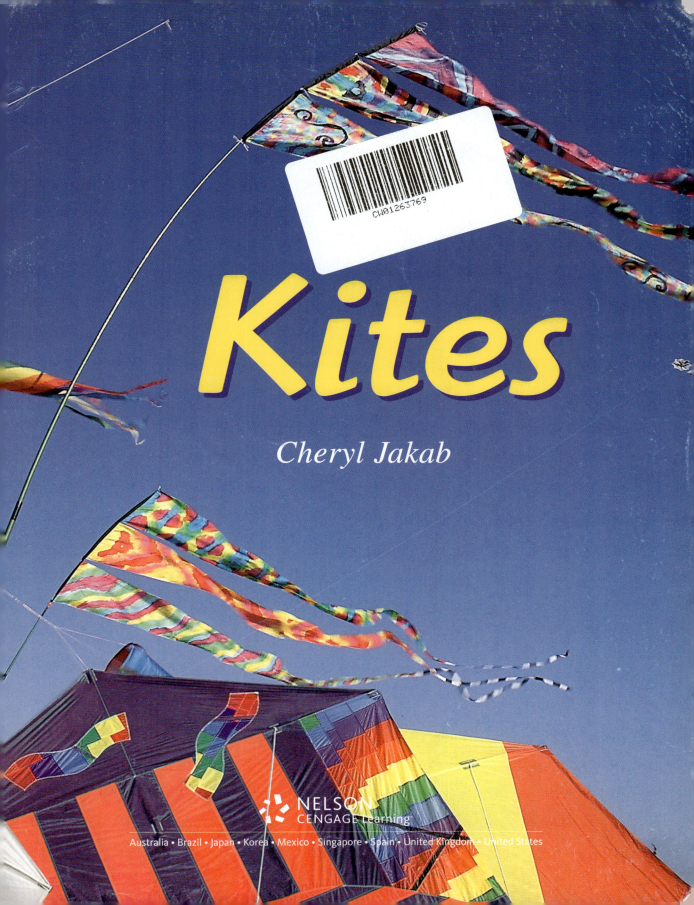

Kites

Cheryl Jakab

NELSON
CENGAGE Learning

Australia • Brazil • Japan • Korea • Mexico • Singapore • Spain • United Kingdom • United States

NELSON
CENGAGE Learning®

Kites

Text: Cheryl Jakab
Text design: Heather Jones
Cover design: Karen Mayo
Illustrations: John Fairbridge
Technology consultant: Cherly Jakab
Typeset in Plantin
Production controller: Siew Han Ong

Acknowledgements
Photos by Australian Picture Library, p. 14 (top)/ Bettmann, p. 8/
Corbis, p. 10/ J. Carnemolla, pp. cover (main), 4–5, 14 (bottom), 22/
Eric Sierins, pp. 5 (right), 6; Robert Soncin Gerometta/ PictureQuest,
p. 23 (bottom); gettyone/ IPL Image Group/ International
Photography Library, pp. imprint, 23 (top); photolibrary.com/ Nick
Green, p. title; Bill Thomas, pp. cover (centre), back cover, 1, 7, 16–21.

PM Non-Fiction
Emerald
Yo-yos
The Pushcart Team
Snowboarding Diary
Skateboarding
Kites
The Bicycle Book

Text © 2001 Cengage Learning Australia Pty Limited
Illustrations © 2001 Cengage Learning Australia Pty Limited

Copyright Notice
This Work is copyright. No part of this Work may be reproduced, stored in a retrieval
system, or transmitted in any form or by any means without prior written permission of
the Publisher. Except as permitted under the *Copyright Act 1968*, for example any fair
dealing for the purposes of private study, research, criticism or review, subject to certain
limitations. These limitations include: Restricting the copying to a maximum of one
chapter or 10% of this book, whichever is greater; Providing an appropriate notice and
warning with the copies of the Work disseminated; Taking all reasonable steps to limit
access to these copies to people authorised to receive these copies; Ensuring you hold
the appropriate Licences issued by the Copyright Agency Limited ("CAL"), supply a
remuneration notice to CAL and pay any required fees.

ISBN 978 1 86 961406 5
ISBN 978 1 86 961400 3 (set)

Cengage Learning Australia
Level 7, 80 Dorcas Street
South Melbourne, Victoria Australia 3205
Phone: 1300 790 853

Cengage Learning New Zealand
Unit 4B Rosedale Office Park
331 Rosedale Road, Albany, North Shore NZ 0632
Phone: 0800 449 725

For learning solutions, visit **cengage.com.au**

Printed in China by 1010 Printing International Ltd
13 14 15 16 17 18 19 19 18 17 16 15

Contents

Chapter 1

Fascinating flyers

Kites are fascinating flying machines. Each year, many kite festivals around the world celebrate the wonders of the kite.

It's easy to see why people love kites. It's a wonderful experience, feeling the wind in your hands and watching your kite skipping, dancing and diving through the air. When in flight, a kite feels more like a living thing than the simple collection of materials that it really is. Once you start flying kites, you may find it hard to stop.

Getting started with kites is easy. But learning about them takes much longer than you might expect.

What do you know about kites?

Chapter 2

Kite tales

No one knows exactly when the first kite was invented. But there are many 'kite tales' that give us hints about their history. Kites have a long history in Asia and the Pacific. People from the islands in the Pacific have used kites to help with fishing since ancient times.

This kite is made out of a palm leaf. It was used as a sail for the boat.

China is widely accepted as the original home of the kite. Over 2000 years ago, the Chinese were making and flying amazing kites. It is said that the Chinese general Huan Theng used a kite to defeat his enemy in 202 BC.

One report suggests that the general was tied to a kite and flown over the enemy camp. He then scared off the enemy by shouting threats at them. Some old Chinese and Japanese prints show warriors being carried by kites.

Chinese kites were originally made out of silk and bamboo.

Kites have also performed some important functions in technology. They have helped scientists perform experiments.

Guglielmo Marconi

In 1901, the inventor of the wireless **telegraph**, Guglielmo Marconi, used a kite to help him 'launch' wireless broadcasting. He did this by using a kite to support an antenna in Newfoundland, North America. The antenna received a signal that came across the ocean from Europe.

In 1847, a bridge was to be built over the gorge of Niagara Falls in North America. The technology to build the bridge existed, but no one knew how to get the first line from one side of the deep gorge to the other. The steep cliffs and mighty rapids, as well as the swirling winds, stopped every attempt. Finally it was suggested that a kite could be used to carry the line. A lot of people attempted to fly a kite across the gorge, but it was 10-year-old Homan Walsh who eventually succeeded in doing this.

Alexander Graham Bell

At the beginning of the 20th century, many scientists tried to achieve heavier-than-air flight. Alexander Graham Bell, who invented the telephone, decided to work on the problem. He designed a kite that was heavy but still flew because of its many small wings. His **tetrahedral** kite showed that heavier-than-air flight is possible.

Chapter 3

Kite design

Although kites were invented long ago, people have not always understood how they work. Identifying the different parts of a kite is a good start to exploring kite designs.

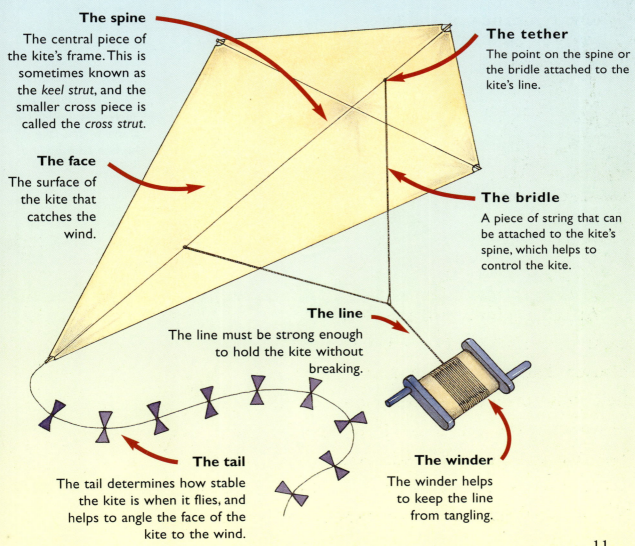

The spine

The central piece of the kite's frame. This is sometimes known as the *keel strut*, and the smaller cross piece is called the *cross strut*.

The face

The surface of the kite that catches the wind.

The tether

The point on the spine or the bridle attached to the kite's line.

The bridle

A piece of string that can be attached to the kite's spine, which helps to control the kite.

The line

The line must be strong enough to hold the kite without breaking.

The tail

The tail determines how stable the kite is when it flies, and helps to angle the face of the kite to the wind.

The winder

The winder helps to keep the line from tangling.

Simple kites are easy to make and fly. Even some of the spectacular kites you see are based on the most simple of designs. But kite designs vary, and slight changes in design can have enormous effects on how a kite flies.

About flight

A well-designed kite depends on the angle it makes to the wind to help it to fly. This angle is called the **attitude** of the kite. The way the kite behaves in the air is called the **aerodynamics** of the kite.

The kite's tail increases the lift by angling the face of the kite to the wind.

The wind presses on the kite's face and creates lift.

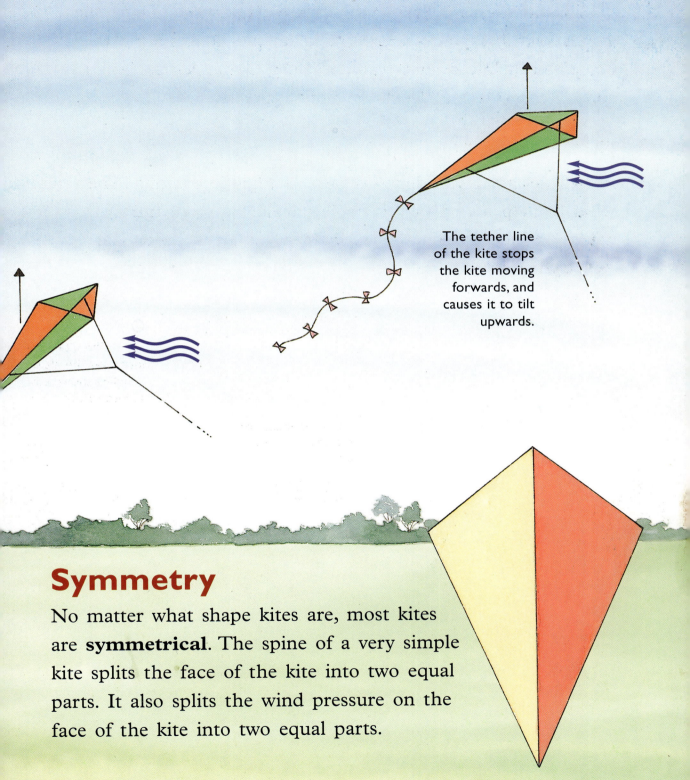

The tether line of the kite stops the kite moving forwards, and causes it to tilt upwards.

Symmetry

No matter what shape kites are, most kites are **symmetrical**. The spine of a very simple kite splits the face of the kite into two equal parts. It also splits the wind pressure on the face of the kite into two equal parts.

Over the years, kites have been built in many shapes and sizes. They can be tiny, such as simple A4-paper kites, or huge monsters that take a team of twenty or more people to fly. However, not all changes in design are intended to make the kites fly better. Kites must look good too!

Chapter 4

Flying a kite

In order to fly properly, a kite needs to have enough lift to overcome **gravity** and **drag**. Keeping the right **tension** on the line is important too. The line should be tight enough to control the kite but loose enough to allow the kite enough **lift** to fly. In strong wind, the kite's tail can be made longer to increase the drag. Almost any kite will fly if the right tether point for the line is found.

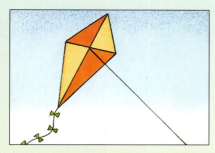

A single-tether kite has one line attached directly to the kite's spine.

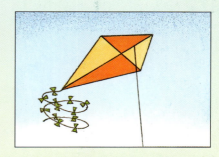

This single-tether line is too high on the spine. The kite will get too much lift.

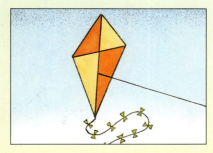

This single-tether line is too low on the spine. The kite will not get enough lift.

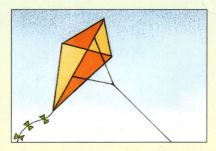

This is a bridle kite. The tether point can be moved up or down according to the wind conditions.

Launching the kite

Face the kite into the wind. Hold it up and let some line out. Pull the line in as the kite starts to lift. If the kite starts to come down, pull the line in a little more. Let out enough line to hold the face of the kite at the right angle to the wind.

Tip

Small kites are suited to light winds and larger kites fly better in strong winds.

Flying the kite

The kite should stay up if you keep the right tension on the line. Tugging and releasing the kite turns it from side to side. Try to feel the patterns of the wind. Even on a still day, you can find little pockets of wind that will help the kite to fly.

Reeling in the kite

The winder is used to reel in the kite. Wind the line around the winder. Sometimes, it can be hard to make a kite come down! If winding in the kite is too hard, ask a friend to walk along the line while leaning on it. The extra weight on the line should bring the kite down while you carefully wind in the line.

Safety first

● When launching and flying a kite, the line can sometimes move very fast. Wearing gloves or using a winder will protect your hands from string burns.

● To fly a kite you need plenty of space away from buildings, trees, roads and powerlines. If your kite touches a powerline, let it go immediately and do not touch it again.

● Never fly a kite in a thunderstorm.

Chapter 5

Making a kite

The diamond kite, or 'two-stick' kite, is probably one of the most famous of all kites. It is also one of the simplest to make, and it is easy to fly.

What you need:

two straight pieces of dowel about 80 cm and 60 cm long

scissors

string

tape

glue

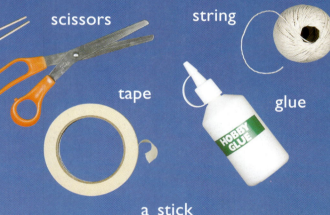

a stick

a sheet of light, but strong paper (about 110 cm x 180 cm)

coloured ribbons or strips of paper

What to do:

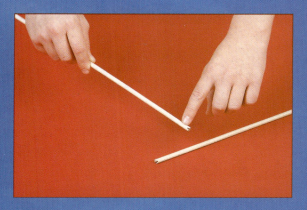

1 Ask an adult to make a deep notch in each end of the dowel sticks. The notches should fall in the same direction.

2 Tie the two sticks together to make a cross. Add tape or a dab of glue to make the joint strong.

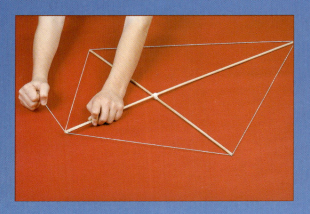

3 Cut a piece of string long enough to make the diamond shape around the kite. Stretch the string around one side of the kite from top to bottom, and then stretch it around the other side of the kite from bottom to top. Make sure the string sits firmly in each notch.

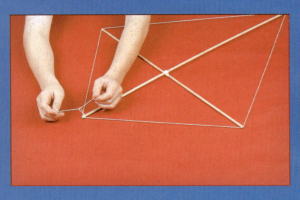

4 Secure the string at the top of the kite by winding it around the stick a few times. The frame must be **taut** but not so tight that the sticks bend.

5 Tape the frame to the paper. Cut the paper about 3 cm larger than the frame. Cut a wedge at each point so the paper folds easily over the frame.

6 Glue the paper to the frame. Leave the glue to dry for a day.

7 Attach coloured ribbons or paper strips to the string to make a tail.

8 Cut a piece of string about 120 cm long and attach the string just above the intersection of the two sticks.

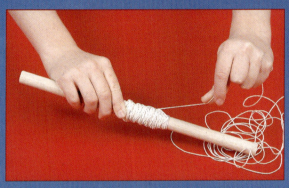

9 Wind the other end of the line around the winder.

Tip

Balance is the most important thing to remember when making your kite. The finished kite must be symmetrical in both shape and weight to fly well.

Chapter 6

Super kites

Today, kites come in a vast array of designs. Modern, lightweight materials allow designers to create wonderful kites. Kite festivals are becoming bigger and better every year. These ancient flying machines have lost none of their fascination over time!

A kite buggy is a three-wheeled vehicle that is steered with the feet. It has no brakes or engine, but is pulled along by a kite. You have to skid or turn to stop or slow the buggy down.

At many kite festivals, big kites are a special feature — really big kites! Two of the biggest kites in the world are known as the Megabyte and the Megaray.

Glossary

aerodynamics   The relationship between an object and the air it moves through.

attitude   The angle of the kite to the wind.

drag   Friction with the air.

gravity   The force that attracts an object towards the centre of the earth, or towards other objects. Gravity causes objects to fall to the ground.

lift   The upward force of wind that raises a kite off the ground.

symmetrical   The same on both sides.

taut   Pulled tight.

telegraph   A device that transmits messages along a wire from one place to another.

tension   The forces tending to stretch an object such as a kite string.

tetrahedral   A kite made up of lots of triangular shapes.

Further reading

Pelham, David, *Kites*, Overlook Press, 2000.

Richardson, J, *Up in the Air, Lift Off Series*, Franklin Watts, Sydney, 1992.

Schmidt, Norman, *The Great Kite Book*, Sterling Publishing, 1998.

Taylor, Barbara, *Air and Flight*, Kingfisher Books, London, 1991.

CW01263725

The Cosmos Collection

To Mum,

Happy B'day!

Sorry I couldn't find MDO, but unearthed this in a book shop in Sheffield. Is a great story, I'd never heard of the place before.

Hope you enjoy.

love John x

ART DECO

NAPIER

styles of the thirties

This book is one in the series
THE COSMOS COLLECTION
concerning the Architectural Heritage
of New Zealand.

Books at present in the series or
in course of preparation include

ART DECO NAPIER - STYLES OF THE THIRTIES
First Edition published by Reed Methuen 1987
Second Edition published by Cosmos Publications 1990
Third Edition published by Craig Potton Publishing 1994

SPANISH MISSION HASTINGS - STYLES OF FIVE DECADES
Published by Cosmos Publications 1991

WHITESTONE OAMARU
To be published 1994

Peter Shaw and Peter Hallett

CRAIG POTTON PUBLISHING

PO Box 555, Nelson, New Zealand

First Published 1987
ISBN 0474 00251 9 (hard cover)

Second Edition Published 1990
ISBN 0 908887 00 0 (hard cover)
ISBN 0 90887 01 9 (soft cover)

Third Edition Published 1994 by
CRAIG POTTON PUBLISHING
PO Box 555, Nelson, New Zealand
in association with
COSMOS PUBLICATIONS
PO Box 5153, Napier, New Zealand
ISBN 0 908802 21 8 (hard cover)
ISBN 0 908802 22 6 (soft cover)

Copyright © Peter Shaw (text), Peter Hallett (photographs)

ALL RIGHTS RESERVED

No part of this publication may be reproduced, stored in a retrieval system or
transmitted in any form or by any means, electronic, mechanical, photocopying,
recording or otherwise without the prior written permission of the Publishers.

Book design by Peter Hallett
Typesetting by Trade & Commerce Centre, Napier
Printed by Kings Time Printing Press, Hong Kong

FOREWORD

In 1982 publication of Heather Ives' *'The Art Deco Architecture of Napier'* by the Ministry of Works & Development began the rapid escalation of awareness and appreciation of Napier's unique buildings. In 1984 the Art Deco Group, now the Art Deco Trust, was formed to work for the preservation and promotion of what they believed to be an architectural collection of world importance, and subsequent events have proved them correct.

Today, visitors from many countries put Napier high on their list of places to see in New Zealand and the attention the buildings receive has encouraged their owners, in most cases, to enhance or restore them and to feel pride in them. In this they have been encouraged by Napier City Council initiatives, in particular the Art Deco Improvement Grant Scheme and the imaginative redevelopment of Emerson Street as a mixed pedestrian and vehicle precinct which complements the inner city's character. The Art Deco Trust, in promoting the city and working with building owners and the Council to protect and enhance its architecture, has also played a major role in increasing both local and international awareness of Napier's architectural heritage.

Publication in 1987 of the First Edition of *'Art Deco Napier - Styles of the Thirties'* by Peter Shaw and Peter Hallett was a landmark in this process of recognition and appreciation and the book has carried all over the world images of Napier's unique mix of styles which forms a tapestry in which all the threads of the Modern Movement are woven together.

This Third Edition of *'Art Deco Napier'* contains many new photographs which record the love and care conferred on the buildings of this small but stunning city since the First Edition appeared and does even greater justice to the visual delights of Napier.

ROBERT McGREGOR
Robert McGregor is Executive Director and
a Founder Member of the Art Deco Trust

PREFACE

This book could never have been written without the help and co-operation of the many Napier people who cheerfully answered questions and allowed us access to their homes and business premises.

No less important is the contribution of others who have written about Napier: Heather Ives with her pioneering book *The Art Deco Architecture of Napier* and Roy Blok, whose unpublished thesis *Salubrious Deco* is held in the Auckland University Library. Jeremy Salmond's *Old New Zealand Houses* provided an invaluable reference as did Geoff Conly's *The Shock of '31* and Dr M D N Campbell's *Story of Napier.*

Film maker Peter Wells was generous with information collected during research for his 1985 film *Newest City on the Globe!* Staff of the Hawke's Bay Museum and Art Gallery, particularly librarian Annette Fairweather, were unfailingly helpful.

There is no doubt that awareness of the value of Napier's unique architectural heritage has greatly increased since 1987 when the first edition of this book appeared. This is outwardly demonstrated in the number of important buildings which have been restored, repainted or improved in other ways whilst at the same time maintaining their original character. We have illustrated some of these in this third edition, replacing earlier photographs with more up to date ones.

The work of the Art Deco Trust has been crucial in increasing the architectural understanding of Napier's residents and visitors alike. Its guided tours of the central city's buildings are both popular and informative; its advice to building owners on colour schemes and associated matters is invaluable.

The positive lead being taken by the Napier City Council in promoting a Heritage Area concept and proposals for the further improvement of the inner city continues to offer encouragement to all who strive for the preservation of Napier's magnificent legacy of the thirties. Their consent to the reproduction of the City Crest in this Edition is greatly appreciated.

Peter Shaw
Peter Hallett
January 1994

"Napier represents the most complete and
significant group of Art Deco buildings in the world,
and is comparable to Bath, England as an example
of a planned townscape in a cohesive style.
NAPIER IS WITHOUT DOUBT UNIQUE."

Dr Neil Cossens OBE MA FSA FMA
Director Science Museum, London
Past President British Museums' Association

art deco napier ~ styles of the thirties

The city of Napier, in New Zealand's Hawke's Bay, has long been renowned for its warm, sunny climate, its seaside location and its Marine Parade lined with Norfolk Island pines.

Advertisers used to call Napier the Nice of the Pacific, hoping to make their city sound as inviting as the French Mediterranean one did to English tourists in the 1870s. New Zealanders as well as foreign travellers journeyed to Napier to stay in its fine hotels, to swim in the famous Salt Water Baths, to stroll in the Botanic Gardens and to listen to the bands playing in the rotunda on Clive Square.

The town's very name called forth comfortingly Imperial associations: Sir Charles Napier had defeated a huge Indian armed force at Meeanee near the city of Hyderabad, India, in 1843. When Alfred Domett was appointed Commissioner of Crown Lands and Resident Magistrate in 1854 he widened these military associations to include his favourite poetic ones. Having already used Clive, Hastings, Scinde and Havelock he decided that the streets should resound with the names of eminent contemporary men of literature and science. Thus they were named Carlyle, Emerson, Dickens, Thackeray, Tennyson, Browning, Faraday and Dalton, Byron, Shakespeare, Milton; Chaucer and Burns added their weight, too. This was necessary, Domett wrote in a letter, because:

> ... it is better to have pleasing associations with the names of our roads and ravines than to be constantly reminded of the existence of obscure individuals (ruffians possibly and runaway convicts) whose names get attached to the places they happen to be the first to pitch upon, and almost to render the places themselves distasteful, however favoured by nature.

Napier, already favoured, was thus rescued from distastefulness and by 1880 presented to the world the perfect image of an English seaside resort.

The Marine Parade at the turn of the century. The Council offices and Courthouse behind the band rotunda are still standing today. The Norfolk Island pines were planted in the early 1890s after the Mayor Mr G H Swan returned from a visit to England, determined to create a 'noble promenade' such as he had seen at English seaside resorts.

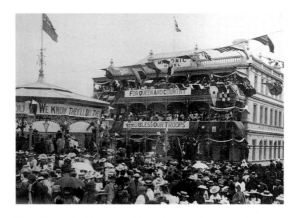

The Masonic Hotel and band rotunda were the scene of the big send-off in 1900 for troops going to the Boer War. One year later, Queen Victoria's memorial service was conducted from the same spot.

A scene of utter devastation - looking northeast from the Holiday Hotel on the corner of Hastings and Dickens Streets. The Post Office clock has stopped at 10:47.

Hawke's Bay's prosperity in the two decades before the turn of the century could be seen at a glance. Large public buildings, extravagantly decorated with wrought iron or moulded concrete, lined the streets. The much-photographed three-storeyed Masonic Hotel was the favourite place to stay. Its tiered balconies were hung with people and signs proclaiming GOD BLESS OUR TROOPS and FOR QUEEN AND COUNTRY on the occasion of the town's farewell to its sons leaving for the Boer War in 1900. They were there again the following year to celebrate the coronation of Edward VII, and again in 1910 for the visit of the Duke and Duchess of York. The architecture and layout of Napier were ideally designed for such grand social occasions.

The growing demand for more impressive buildings provided work for an English architect, Robert Lamb, who had originally come to Napier on account of ill health. Among other things, he designed a Marine Parade frontage very much along the lines of the English south coast city of Brighton. Although his designs were never built, they show that the image of Napier as an English seaside town was in the forefront of people's minds. It was also in the mind of whoever wrote the Hawke's Bay Motor Company's 1912 *Guide to Napier,* describing "the arrival in summer of families who came from the back country to seek the cooling breezes of the Pacific and a delicious plunge in the bright salt waves."

Visitors still enjoy all the pleasures available to the Victorian traveller in Napier, but the city now has a significant new claim to fame - its unique mixture of architectural styles. In fact few of the structures that graced the Victorian town by the sea remain; today Napier presents a quite different face to its visitors. The English-inspired colonial buildings have mostly disappeared and the modern city has a distinctly Californian appearance. Some call it the Art Deco Capital of the World – an exaggeration, but not altogether inappropriate.

Tuesday, 3 February 1931, was a disastrous day for the seaside town. It was hot and dry at a quarter to eleven in the morning – "real earthquake weather," as they still say – when suddenly the earth started to sway violently. People had begun tentatively to settle down again, when a terrific downward moving twist was felt, followed by the same swaying motion. In just two and a half minutes Napier crumbled to ruins.

Then a brisk easterly wind sprang up, spreading flames from the fires in two chemists' shops, one in Hastings Street and the other at the back of the Masonic Hotel. Because the earthquake had destroyed almost all of the town's water pipes, the fire brigade's efforts were severely hampered. Although an area along Hastings, Munroe and Carlyle Streets was saved, next morning only the Public

Trust office, Dalgety's Building and the Hawke's Bay Motor Company remained standing.

The earthquake registered 7.9 on the Richter scale and 258 people lost their lives, a high proportion of them killed by masonry falling from buildings decorated with overhanging ornamental parapets and pediments. Evacuation began on 4 February when the Mayor of Palmerston North notified the hastily-formed Napier Citizens' Control Committee that his borough's relief centre could take 5,000 refugees. Women and children went immediately; men were expected to stay.

The town's water reservoir had fallen across the croquet lawn in Thompson Road, drenching the players, so 400-gallon tanks mounted on lorries were filled from artesian wells in McLean Park. Barrels located at prominent places were kept filled for householders who collected water in jugs and buckets. Sewerage was a major problem, electricity less so. After two steel transmission towers had been repaired, Napier received power from Waikaremoana the weekend after the earthquake.

The centre of Napier after the earthquake - the Public Trust Office at right was one of the few buildings still standing.

Rushed immediately to the scene, a special reporter from *The Dominion* Wellington, told his story:

> Shrouded with a pall of evil-smelling smoke, Napier has become overnight a skeleton of its former self and the grave of what remains an indeterminate number of its population of 20,000 persons. With one gigantic sweep the earthquake has reduced the whole town to a heap of ruins, still blazing and crumbling at each shake. The population has become a community without a home, without food and water, and for the most part without shelter. In one moment, so sudden was the visitation, the population was divorced from its town, to become, as it were, a thing apart from the mass of buildings that joined in one great conflagration from end to end of the business area. Napier as a town has become wiped off the map. Today it is a smouldering heap of ruins, the sepulchre of a prosperous port and the gaunt remains of a beautiful seaside town.

The Rehabilitation Committee worked with the Earthquake Relief Committee to organise the reoccupation of damaged houses. Each had one chimney repaired free of charge but many owners felt understandably reluctant to reoccupy as the succession of aftershocks continued in the weeks after 3 February. Lists of tent dwellers in Nelson Park were made, their homes checked and gentle persuasion applied to encourage them to return.

After one enterprising shop keeper put up the first "Business as Usual" sign there was a rush to resume commercial activity. By Tuesday 10 February, the Prime Minister, Mr Forbes and his cabinet were in Napier to see for themselves. Fifty MPs came on a special overnight train on 1 March, while the Governor-General, Lord Bledisloe and his wife arrived by special vice-regal railcar on the 7th.

As a result of their observations the Government announced a loan of £10,000 for the building of 54 temporary business premises in Clive Square and Memorial Square. "Tin Town" opened on 16 March. The first temporary building to appear after the earthquake was the Fletcher Construction Company's office block for "Associated Banks", in which an unusual association of rival banks was temporarily established. After five weeks the Control Committee was disbanded and the former Napier Borough Council's functions transferred to a Government Commission of two men: John S Barton, a magistrate, and Lachlan B Campbell, inspecting engineer to the Public Works Department.

'Tin Town' - temporary shops erected in Clive and Memorial Squares.

Because the Napier earthquake occurred when the worldwide Great Depression was beginning to be felt in New Zealand, the Government's grant only amounted to one-fifth of the estimated losses in Napier. Requests for loans to enable rebuilding were dealt with by the Rehabilitation Committee which insisted that all national and international firms, banks, insurance companies and mercantile houses, finance their own reconstruction. For the others, loans were granted interest-free for periods of one to three years, after which borrowers paid 4½%. Many found this a heavy burden as they were already paying off pre-earthquake mortgages.

When the two commissioners turned their attention to the central business district they consulted the Napier Reconstruction Committee. This had been formed in July 1931, meeting in the Trocadero Tearooms, Hastings Street, to deal with all matters pertaining to architectural design, street widening, town planning and building location.

The widening of the town's main thoroughfare, Emerson Street, had started before the earthquake, after property owners agreed to allow three metres to be taken from their land. Now the committee added Tennyson, Thackeray and Waghorne Streets and Church Lane to the widening programme. All street corners were to be splayed, power and telephone lines put underground, stormwater and sewer lines placed under footpaths, verandahs suspended rather than supported by posts and verandah depths made uniform. Service lanes behind shops and dividing the inner-city blocks were approved and a uniform two-storey height restriction imposed.

The Napier Reconstruction Committee got through a vast amount of business. It dealt with crucial issues of public health such as hospital rebuilding, clearing of debris using unemployed labour and building inspection. It found time, on 22 July 1931, to depute to Mr H Anderson (of the Business and Property Owners Association) and Mr M S Spence (representing local accountants), the task of "drawing up a letter to Mr Rockefeller, congratulating him upon reaching such an advanced age and forwarding particulars, accompanied by pictures depicting the damage done to Napier by the earthquake. It is hoped by this means to enlist his practical sympathy." It also entered into lengthy discussions about the future of the Marine Parade foreshore. The inevitable subcommittee was formed to consider possible improvements.

The image of Napier as an English seaside resort did not entirely crumble in 1931 with the town's buildings. The Napier-born but London-trained architect Stanley Natusch, although long an advocate of street widening, believed that

The Napier Reconstruction Committee.
Back Row: A Mayne, A B Hurst, P W Peters, H Anderson, R M Chadwick, K McLeay, L Hay
Front Row: T M Geddis, Dr Fitzgerald, W G Martin, M S Spence, L Pickering, M R Grant

Looking along the rebuilt Tennyson Street. At left the Sainsbury, Logan & Williams Building is complete. Across the road from left, so are the Masonic Hotel and Market Reserve Building, although scaffolding still surrounds Bowman's building and the Kaiapoi Woollen Mills Building.

'Anything but uniform' - Hastings Street displays three of Louis Hay's 'Chicago School' buildings, (left to right) Abbott's Building, Parker's Chambers and F Thorp & Co. Spanish touches are apparent above Azzopardi & Holland, Opticians, alongside a line of Art Deco detailing above the windows of the building next door.

there was little need for radical change to the essential appearance of the central business district. "The original town plan of Napier was quite sound and on reasonably good lines," he later observed cautiously in the *New Zealand institute of Architects Journal* of April 1933.

As a member of the Marine Parade Subcommittee he also favoured the idea, eventually adopted, of putting debris from demolished buildings along the seafront, creating a garden esplanade beneath the Norfolk Island pines. When an official of the Parks and Gardens Department objected that aggressive, salt-laden winds would quickly destroy the plants, Natusch's reply was simple and typical: "Remember Torquay" – that English town being famous for its gardens. The architect J A Louis Hay drew up plans for an elaborate entertainment centre and later designed a magnificent Albion Hotel for the Parade. Alas, neither was ever built.

Hay provided liaison between the Reconstruction Committee, of which he was a foundation member, and the Associated Architects of Napier. Burying the rivalry usually found between different architectural practices, especially in small towns, the Associated Architects comprised C T Natusch and Sons, Finch and Westerholm, J A Louis Hay and E A Williams. The volume of work in the period of reconstruction was so great that it became necessary for these separate firms to operate as a design collective on some jobs. The Associated Architects also lobbied those in positions of power to ensure that local architects rather than outsiders got the jobs.

There was of course, much discussion of the new Napier's appearance. On 4 February the *Daily Telegraph* reported that:

> Napier has object lessons in other cities which have been laid waste by quake and fire and have been rebuilt to greater magnificence and grandeur than ever before. Napier people are determined that they will do the same.

In 1925 the Californian city of Santa Barbara had suffered a serious earthquake but had since been rebuilt in a predominantly Spanish style, as befitted its Hispanic origins. On 16 February, the *Daily Telegraph,* under the headline *Buildings of a Uniform Style,* proclaimed:

> The attractiveness of Santa Barbara, one of the youngest yet most beautiful cities of California, is behind the suggestion that all permanent buildings erected in Napier of the future should conform to a uniform style of architecture. A handful of enthusiasts are working unobtrusively in the advancement of the proposal and have

already succeeded in exciting and encouraging interest among architects in the city, who share the advocacy of the Spanish style of architecture, and which is favoured for its multifarious advantages, notably economy, simplicity and safety.

Photographs and information arrived from Santa Barbara, which also appropriately shared with Napier a long, uninterrupted, tree-lined foreshore.

The talented American architect R A Lippincott, associate of Walter Burley Griffin and resident in Auckland since 1921, also supported the idea, agreeing that the elements of Santa Barbara's post-earthquake problems were identical with Napier's. "Santa Barbara", he observed, "instead of being a heterogeneous collection of unrelated buildings, each swearing at the other, has risen from her ruins."

By June 1931 a plan had appeared for the construction of one large building along Emerson Street, all the way from Hastings Street to Dalton Street, with an upper storey set ten feet back, providing a Spanish-style arcade/boulevard along the length of the block. It never eventuated because, in the depressed economic climate, finance was not available to allow the creation of a uniform Spanish style modelled on Santa Barbara. But the Spanish Mission style is significantly represented in the Napier of today.

The modern appearance of the city is anything but uniform, despite the hopes of those in the forefront of reconstruction after the earthquake. Such was the urgency to get the town going again that there was no time for the protracted discussion of aesthetic matters required for the realisation of that dream.

But one thing is certain – the rebuilders of Napier in 1931 offered a clean slate, turned not to England for their inspiration but to America. Disaster had been visited unexpectedly upon their town but social ideals remained unchanged. In fact the alterations to Napier's town plan were merely cosmetic; no-one felt the need for drastic change despite the unique opportunity. The citizens of Napier wished to resurrect their town, not to revolutionise its appearance.

Napier, the Victorian town, had gone forever. England offered no inspiration in 1931 but the architectural journals from America were full of new and interesting ideas which Napier's architects were keen to adopt in the challenge of reconstructing their city. Louis Hay was already a fervent admirer of the great Chicago architect Louis Sullivan (1856-1924) and of Frank Lloyd Wright (1869-1959). Some of the first graduates of the Auckland University School of Architecture, grateful for an escape route from the dole queues, came straight to Napier, where they were given plenty of opportunity to work in the modern

A revealing comparison can be made between the forms and motifs used on these pieces of jewellery, a Clarice Cliff 'Bizarre' Tea Set and those found in Napier's Art Deco architecture.

COLLECTION OF THE HAWKE'S BAY CULTURAL TRUST
HAWKE'S BAY MUSEUM

styles familiar to them from such widely read American magazines as *Pencil Points* and *The Architectural Record*.

For these architects Napier was indeed, as Peter Wells' 1985 film so clearly showed, the *Newest City on the Globe!* The city was to be modern in the American way and that meant what we now know as Art Deco.

Writing in *Pencil Points* in December 1930, W Franklin Paris found the origins of the new style in a reaction against Art Nouveau which was, he said,

> ... cloyed with ornamentation based on botanical themes. Now in England, Belgium, France and Germany, was dawning the realisation of a new beauty – the beauty of simplicity ... the eyes rested gratefully on plain surfaces, well proportioned and logically disposed. In Germany, industry allied itself to art. This cooperation, originating in Munich in 1907, bound together in a common effort some 800 craftsmen and manufacturers and resulted in the sensational exhibition of the Munich school held in Paris in 1910. Paris the year before had been agreeably shocked by the new colour values revealed by the Russian Ballet with its gorgeous settings by Leon Bakst.

This new modernist energy was dispersed by World War I but revived again in the 1919 Paris Exhibition of Decorative Arts. Franklin Paris wrote,

> It was not until 1924 that the attention of the entire world found itself focused on Modern Art. In that year the French organised and held the International Exposition of Decorative Arts and definitely established the new doctrine. The Exposition made history. It was epochal in character and revolutionary in many of its effects. Its exhibits have been dispersed and its temporary structures demolished but no-one can really understand the present trend without studying it in detail.

The 1925 Paris Exhibition, *L'Exposition Internationale des Arts Decoratifs et Industriels Modernes*, was a lavish affair. Dominated by fine and detailed craftsmanship, it displayed objects and furnishings exquisitely wrought in ivory, Macassar ebony, silk brocade, Caucasian walnut, pale sycamore, chrome and opalescent glass. Today books on Art Deco style (the term did not exist in 1925) reproduce photographs of these dazzling objects with their stylised curves, geometrical ornamentation, primitive allusions and rich colour.

American designers in Paris for the Exposition took the new style back to New York and adapted it for their wealthy clients who wanted something exclusive, luxurious and modern. Others were determined to popularise the "modernistic". Department store buyers, fashion designers and decorators translated the new style into something more appropriate for the public purse and taste. As Martin Greif writes in his *Depression Modern:*

> Characterised generally by zigzags and asymmetrical patterning, it reduced the wealth and endless variety of Art Deco to a handful of decorative motifs, a squiggle here, a stylised sunburst there ... by 1930 the modernistic filled the lobbies of New York hotels and skyscrapers.

The style we now call Art Deco changed further as the result of the constraints of the worldwide Depression. It became simpler, less extravagant, clean and uncluttered. Decoration on the predominantly large, flat, plain surfaces of buildings was limited to bas-relief bands of incised abstract motifs frequently derived from plant forms.

American architectural magazines dispersed information about the modern style of building all over the world, including to New Zealand. In October 1929 *The Architectural Record* carried an article called *Small Shops* by the designer J R Davidson. One year later an article entitled *A Portfolio of Banks* appeared in the same magazine. "Similarities in treatment of exteriors, whether in this country or in Panama or South America, are readily apparent", wrote the Editor. The National City Bank of New York, in Brooklyn, or another on the corner of 34th Street and 7th Avenue, or indeed the Panama or Buenos Aires branches, could all be suitably transported to Napier without any clash of style. This was an international style.

Napier's best Art Deco buildings are rather fewer in number than is generally believed, mainly because people have tended to describe the buildings in the whole of the city's central business district as Art Deco. But Spanish Mission-style work done by Finch and Westerholm is not Art Deco; neither are the Chicago School buildings designed by J A Louis Hay under the influence of Louis Sullivan or Frank Lloyd Wright.

However, the Central Hotel, designed by E A Williams for the Napier Brewery Company in 1931, has many classic Art Deco features. It was conceived as a solid block forming the corner of Emerson and Dalton Streets, the centre of which is a triple-bayed, octagonally arched balcony. The mouldings of each arch have been flattened and covered with a variety of geometric patterns, among them the popular sunburst motif.

In bas-relief right around the top of the building, including the central bay, is the zigzag/chevron motif. This motif occurs again and again in Art Deco buildings

The new Emerson Street in the thirties.

Clean lines and symmetrical decoration - looking towards the Central Hotel from Dalton Street.

the world over but no-one is quite sure where it comes from. Many architects would have seen it used on Ely Jacques Kahn's Insurance Centre Building of 1926, in New York, but Kahn himself said that he borrowed the motif from textile patterns.

Inside, the same zigzag/chevron motif runs along the scotia while faceted pillars are ornamented with the sharply broken up geometrical patterns to be found on the central bay's verandah. The architect has brought his external octagonal patterns and sunbursts indoors, weaving them into green, red and gold leadlight windows, skylights, banisters and doors. It is unfortunate that natural veneer wall panels have been painted a soft grey and elaborately stepped plaster cornices have been picked out in a particularly harsh shade of pink.

Diagonally across the road lies the extraordinary Kidson's Corner, originally designed as the Smith and Chambers Building in 1932 by H Alfred Hill. It does not curve around the corner site, but moves in a series of flat planes decorated with the zigzag as well as simple linear motifs which help to tie the various facets together. This building has been sympathetically painted, thus allowing its Art Deco features to be easily read from the street.

E A Williams also designed the Daily Telegraph Building in Tennyson Street. It, too, presents a symmetrical face to the street, again distinguished by a central bay which contains a balcony at first floor level and the main entrance doors at the ground floor. The zigzag appears around the entrance in raised wrought iron. The building's stripped classical symmetry is emphasised by pilasters placed at regular intervals across the facade, each capital decorated at the top with heavily stylised leaf forms. On spandrels between the pillars a small decorative motif subtly binds the whole structure together.

Originally the single storeyed building was lit from above by leadlight and glass block skylights enclosed within coffered spaces and decorated with bas-relief zigzag patterns. Today, with the addition of a mezzanine floor, the dramatic light effects of these incised patterns around the skylight, when viewed from far below, has been lost as the viewer is forced to stand much closer than the designer intended.

Then there is the Marine Parade's Masonic Hotel built in 1932 to a design by the Wellington architect W J Prouse. It is an extremely simple, symmetrical concrete structure, enlivened only by its elaborate upper-storey wooden pergola facing the sea, and its conspicuously Deco overhanging pediment above a suspended glass and metal verandah which proclaims the word "Masonic" in Deco capitals of red leadlight. The building's long, low-lying aspect is emphasised

The interior of the Daily Telegraph offices in their original splendour.

by incised parallel lines which run along above and below the set-in windows.

The hotel's once splendid interior can now only be glimpsed by peering at a faded colour print kept inside a glass case in the foyer. Since the 1970s paint has obscured much of the fine Art Deco plaster work in the dining room and extensive alterations in what is now a bar area have since been carried out.

Standing outside in Herschell Street under the pohutukawas one can look along the facade and experience the illusion that the magnificent Temperance & General Building with its "lighthouse" tower is part of the Masonic. The A & B, as it is now known, was also designed in Wellington, by Atkins and Mitchell. Its stripped and undecorated curving form reaches upward to a tower complete with Renaissance drum, dome and lantern. Instead of beckoning ships out at sea this "lighthouse" offers an illuminated clock to the citizens of Napier.

The image of the city building as a lighthouse had been seen in New York's Singer and Metropolitan Life buildings of 1899 and 1893. There is another "lighthouse" on the path outside the former Ministry of Works building and another, even smaller, on the lawn outside a house in Tom Parker Avenue, Marewa.

Following the recent conversion of the first floor of the A & B building into a Conference Centre, it is possible to see again Napier's only 1930's lift and the decorative plaster work on the walls of the stairways.

Before the earthquake, the area between the sea and the Masonic Hotel formed the Victorian public square of Napier. After the band rotunda and the Masonic crumbled in 1931 the Boer War monument was moved there from its original site following a call from an honest Invercargill commercial traveller who had had the misfortune to be in the town on 3 February and had temporarily souvenired the statue's head.

Across the road are the three Memorial Arches designed by J T Watson to commemorate the new Napier and two of its citizens, Robert C Wright and Harold Latham. The Sound Shell, financed by a long-established local service organisation, the Thirty Thousand Club, is situated at the southern end, facing what was originally an outdoor skating rink with inlaid Art Deco designs in the concrete surface.

Louis Hay's grandiose entertainment centre was too expensive to build but council and club funds contributed to the Sun Bay or sea colonnade where in later years the bell of *HMS Veronica* was hung to commemorate the invaluable work done by the ship's company in the aftermath of the earthquake. In 1990 after dangerous weaknesses were discovered in its concrete foundation work,

One of the two Art Deco pediments over the entrance doors of the Masonic Hotel.

In commemoration of the invaluable help given by the crew of HMS Veronica in the days immediately following the earthquake, the Ship's Bell was installed on the Colonnade in 1935.

the Sun Bay was demolished and completely rebuilt to the original design.

Soundshells were another expression of that Art Deco fixation, the sunburst. First created by Samuel L Rothafel as a form for theatrical performances, his soundshells were designed as a series of consecutive plaster semicircles. In the case of New York's famous Radio City Music Hall, these were painted gold to reflect the colours of the lights, but Napier's was constructed of timber for acoustic reasons.

Further along the gardens is the fountain presented to the city in 1936 by Mr Tom Parker, a local men's outfitter. He had been to the English seaside town of Bournemouth, where he particularly enjoyed the play of a similar illuminated fountain in which colour and spray flow were interestingly varied.

Mention must be made of the magnificent ASB Bank building on the corner of Hastings and Emerson Street. Originally designed for the Bank of New Zealand by the Wellington firm of Crichton, McKay and Haughton in 1932, it has many typical Art Deco features on its exterior. The stripped facade is decorated with incised panels featuring not the usual Art Deco motifs but designs drawn from Maori art. This building has been tattooed – a veritable Bank of Aotearoa.

Its designers exploited the obvious similarity between the Art Deco zigzag and a kowhai pattern on the lintels above the main entrance and borrowed from a carving pattern a motif used at the tops of the pilasters. The Maori influence continues in the interior of the bank where another kowhaiwhai decorates cornices and panels around the superb coffered ceiling's skylights. A mask from the head of a taiaha gazes down at the bank's customers from the main corners – the use of Maori motifs throughout the building underlines the essential New Zealand quality of the bank.

The one-storeyed Ross and Glendinning building in Cathedral Lane, now Whitehouse Interiors, also has a frieze derived from a rafter pattern based on the pitau or fern frond, although recent redecoration here has largely destroyed the power of the original design when painted in traditional Maori red and black. The use of motifs drawn from earlier cultures as diverse as Egyptian and pre-Columbian was an important characteristic of Art Deco design from 1925 onwards, and Napier's two Maori-decorated structures are well within that tradition of assimilating the primitive into the modern.

Louis Hay's original prizewinning design for the Municipal Theatre in Tennyson Street was rejected as too expensive after lengthy and acrimonious debate, and the present structure wasn't opened until 1938. It is the work of J T Watson, the City Architect. The building is an extraordinary blend of decorative influences which nonetheless combine into a pleasing whole. On the street, two squat, distinctly Egyptian-looking pillars divide the three sets of double doors. When these are closed the metal handles make a neat geometric pattern against the glass and stained wood. The foyer lit with coloured glass lights reflects the strongly favoured mechanical analogy which was such an important part of the Art Deco visual aesthetic A curved, walnut-veneered ticket box, chrome strips decorating the front of the circle and wall lights extending out of chrome strips give the interior more than a hint of the streamlined Deco rarely found in Napier but which is a feature of cinemas in some other New Zealand cities.

The auditorium is floodlit by variously coloured lights cast from an elaborate central dome. Above the two side-exit doors large, symmetrically-shaped arched panels depict a leaping naked woman whose drapery forms a swirling pattern. This dancing woman was a very popular image of the time, cast in anything from bronze to plastic, and could be found on lamp stands, cigarette cases and clocks. Art Deco was, among other things, concerned with movement, with what the Futurist architectural manifesto called "a taste for light, practical forms, for the provisional, for rapidity." This interest in the mobile and the dynamic encompassed both natural and mechanical qualities; many of the stripped-back, smooth or aggressively angular forms of Art Deco buildings owe their appearance to the shapes of machine forms. During the Depression there wasn't the money in Napier to permit elaborate expression of these characteristic forms, but part of the city's uniqueness lies in the small-scale versions of styles more grandly realised overseas.

To call Napier an Art Deco city is merely to give a convenient label to a city which contains the buildings of an architect whose work draws on a whole range of styles quite different from those which have their origin in the Paris Exhibition of 1925.

J A Louis Hay (1881-1948) was a man of wide interests and accomplishments, a fine flautist, water skier, boat builder, sailor and actor. He remains in the memory of many who knew him as a genial fellow, though capable of stern decisions when the occasion demanded. He is still remembered for his treatment of those builders who tried, but failed, to get away with shoddy workmanship. Hay's earliest work in Napier dates from 1911 and was mostly domestic. Very few of these houses were destroyed in the earthquake because most of them were situated "on the hill" or outside Napier as far south as Hatuma, near Waipukurau. All show considerable influence from the English Arts and Crafts movement and particularly the work of Voysey, Lethaby and Baillie Scott. The enormous 7,500

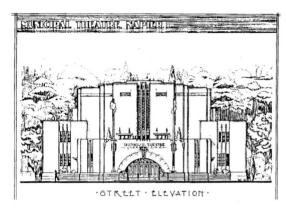

This street elevation of Louis Hay's original drawing of his proposed design for the Municipal Theatre has been reconstructed from a photograph by Adrian Robinson.

The Hannah house (1914) as it originally appeared before the verandah was filled in and another storey added.
(Below) The imposing stone entrance. Both these photographs come from Louis Hay's own album.

square-foot Frank Lloyd Wright-style house *Waiohika* (1920) outside Gisborne is Hay's most distant building.

Hay owned the two large portfolios of Frank Lloyd Wright's early Chicago buildings published by Wasmuth of Berlin in 1910 and 1911. These were to remain a lifelong inspiration to him, although his greatest Frank Lloyd Wright-derived building, the opulent 1933 Albion Hotel, was never completed. The architect's repeated efforts to interest brewery companies in both Australia and New Zealand met with no success.

Another house, *Mornington*, in Sealy Road, displays all the typical elements of Hay's California bungalow style. Built in 1921 for Mr John Walker Findlay, the house is named after the Dunedin suburb where the owner was born. *Mornington* shares with most of Hay's houses on the hill a long, low profile, a preference for casement windows and pergola verandahs, exposed rock construction (both exterior and interior), and a low, wide eaves line to give shade from the bright Napier sun. This latter feature clearly derives from the American Prairie house which flattened the more distinctively English high gable seen in the houses of Lutyens, Baillie Scott and C F A Voysey.

Two houses side by side in Fitzroy Road are fine examples of Hay's early work. Two young sisters, Mrs Lila Hannah and Miss Doris Dolbel commissioned him, in 1914 and 1918 respectively, to design houses for them; the backs of both sections were connected by a tennis court.

The Hannah house exhibits the characteristic low horizontal line, though the main feature of the structure is a false arch-chimney form which acts as main entry and binds the two roof planes together. Many of Frank Lloyd Wright's Prairie houses have a central anchoring chimney form which also performs the function of firmly connecting the building to the ground. *Mornington* does this too, its hilly site requiring a huge amount of stone from the nearby Coote Road quarry.

The Dolbel house boasts a magnificent pergola-type stone verandah and inside, red, white and blue geometric leadlights which Hay designed in clear emulation of Wright's work in the 1903 Susan Lawrence Dana house in Springfield, Illinois. This house was obviously a favourite of Hay's and he frequently borrowed from it details of roofing, verandah and fireplace construction as well as leadlight design. Increasingly, too, he favoured its more open planned approach to room functions, using sliding doors to permit freer access from sitting to dining rooms.

Like Wright, Louis Hay insisted on using the finest materials inside his houses. He usually specified heart rimu woodwork and invariably designed a scheme of leadlight windows to suit each individual client's tastes. These ranged in style from the most sinuous Art Nouveau floral forms to the severely geometric, clearly influenced by similar work of Frank Lloyd Wright.

Hay's commercial buildings are some of Napier's finest. In the central business district the AMP building shows his abiding enthusiasm for the work of the great Chicago architect Louis Sullivan. Built by W M Angus Ltd, it is a steel-framed, two-storeyed structure designed to satisfy the new laws governing earthquake-resisting construction.

Here Louis Hay indulged many of his architectural enthusiasms, creating a beautifully unified structure out of a collection of different influences. Derived from Sullivan is the arched main entrance on Shakespeare Road, decorated with bunches of grapes combined with elaborate leafy motifs. The other door, originally that of the Queensland Insurance Company, is even more spectacular in conception. In contrast with the semi-circular one beside it, it is clearly derived from the step-like vertical structures of Mayan architecture which was such an important source of Art Deco ideas. Here, too, tendrils derived from plant forms are placed so as to clarify further the geometrical design of the whole door. Ornamental designs in moulded concrete on cornices above windows, running almost continuously around the parapet, are discreetly placed on large flat surface areas, as they are in Louis Hay's Hildebrandt Building (1932) and on those which feature the Wright-derived jagged sculpted concrete patterns Hay so often used. From Wright's 1903 Larkin Building in Buffalo came the design of the wall bracket light fittings - sadly only two remain today, installed on either side of an upstairs reception counter.

Now the property of Callinicos Gallagher, lawyers, the building has been painstakingly restored by its new owners to the original Hay plan, the work including re-siting the staircase to its original position and dismantling interior partitioning. Publicity given to this work whilst it was in progress led to some of the original doors and other important items coming to light. These have been included in the building's restoration based on an examination of the architect's own photographs taken shortly after it was opened in 1933.

While never aspiring to the extremes Wright went to in his 1920 Aline Barnsdall *Hollyhock* house in California, there is a close resemblance between Wright's concrete decoration and Louis Hay's. Examples of these can be found on such buildings as the Munster and Tennyson Chambers (1932), designed by

Louis Hay's own album of photographs of the newly constructed AMP Building in 1933 contains this image of the arcaded staircase alcove inside the Browning Street entrance. It can be compared with the 1993 restoration illustrated on page 66.

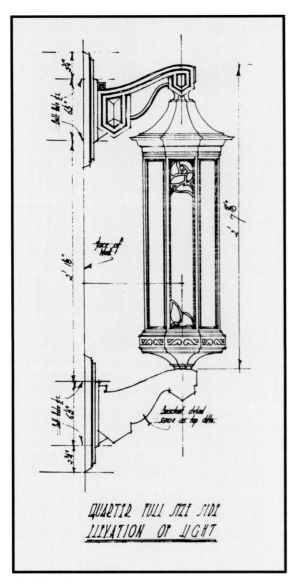

QUARTER FULL SIZE SIDE
ELEVATION OF LIGHT

This light fitting for the facade of Louis Hay's
National Tobacco Company Building was drawn and
traced by Leonard J Wolfe - it typifies the attention
given to detail in an elaborately conceived building.

Louis Hay in conjunction with C T Natusch and Sons; Abbotts Building (1932), with J B Frame; and the 1931 Napier Fire Station (now the Desco Building). The sadly neglected little Ellison and Duncan Building at Ahuriri, which has been deprived of its Union Street frontage and swallowed up into a cartage contractor's yard, is a particularly fine example.

Louis Hay's best-known building is the National Tobacco Company of 1934, now owned by Rothmans. In this Hay employed the distinctly Sullivanesque scheme of placing an arch within a cube, in accordance with the wishes of his client, Mr Gerhard Husheer, that the building be simple in form yet highly decorated.

Hay had already remodelled three houses at the end of Elizabeth Road on Bluff Hill for this wealthy client. He had had leadlight designs returned to him by Husheer on the grounds that they weren't elaborate enough. The National Tobacco Company building shows no such restraint, covered as it is with cleverly placed clumps of sculpted roses. On either side of the doors, carved by Gwen Nelson of Havelock, the roses are combined with raupo into a pleasing but unlikely arrangement. The two piers of the arch display the Art Deco undulating wave motif Hay had already used on the Hildebrandt Building. Vine leaves and bunches of grapes also feature.

The gleaming brasswork of the banisters, the rich woodwork of the doors, the ornate lamps and the speckled marble foyer with its beautiful glass dome make this Napier's most luxurious post-earthquake building. The Depression was an irrelevance to Hay's client.

Although they are important in number and scale, Napier's Spanish-style buildings are often overlooked in the enthusiasm for the more obviously Art Deco structures. It is entirely appropriate that a city with a climate as warm and sunny as Napier's should include a Mediterranean element, albeit derived from the Spanish Mission style of California. This arose in California during the 1890's as the result of concern that the Spanish missions of the eighteenth century were in danger of collapsing completely.

The imagery for the twentieth-century revival of Spanish Mission-style derives from buildings such as the Mission San Luis Rey de Francia in San Diego County. Here was the *espadana* or curved parapet, the adobe look of white plaster or stucco, the varicoloured tile work, the arches, the twisted columns. The first major building in the new style had been the Californian Building at the World's Columbian Exposition at Chicago in 1893. It was designed by the San Francisco architect A Page Brown and modelled after the missions of Santa Barbara and San

Diego. All these elements, much-illustrated in architectural periodicals of the late twenties and early thirties, transferred easily to Napier. While there was little need or money for the extravagant *campanario,* or bell tower, of the Spanish missions, Louis Hay used this feature in miniature in his very few Spanish-style buildings such as the Napier Club.

The major exponent of the Spanish-style in Napier was the firm of Finch and Westerholm, which designed the ABH Building as premises for Mrs S Williams (1932), C E Rogers and Co (1932), the Provincial Hotel (1932), the now demolished UFS Dispensary (1931) and the State Cinema (1933). The Spanish-style was also utilised by C T Natusch and Sons in their McGruer's building (1932) and by E A Williams for his large-scale Criterion Hotel (1932) and also Harstons which was built in 1930 and strengthened after the earthquake. Nearly all of these have a centrally placed group of three windows as in the Central Hotel, except that in Spanish Mission-style buildings the windows are often separated by twisted columns. The plastered white surfaces are usually capped by tilted cordova terracotta half-tiles where cornices would once have been.

Many Napier architectural firms employed students who had just graduated from the School of Architecture at Auckland University. The sheer volume of work done in the years 1931 and 1932 meant that tracing, measuring up, and drawing details, especially of decorative motifs, had to be delegated by the firms' principals. The very real contribution of these young men to the final appearance of Napier is frequently overlooked. To a large extent it was they who chose and then drew up the ornamentation for a particular facade. They knew the "modern look" and were pleased to have the opportunity of putting their newly-learned skills to immediate practical use.

Men such as F Kingwell Malcolm (who worked for both Finch and Westerholm and E A Williams at different times in the thirties), J Hall-Kenny, Arthur Marshall, Charles Corne, Arthur Milne, Euan Wainscott, Graham Fox, Charles Crookes, Wilfred Bedford and Leonard J Wolfe worked for long hours in the city's main architectural practices. Many of them went on to become prominent architects in cities all over New Zealand.

Kingwell Malcolm remembers that "Westy", as H A Westerholm was commonly known, was something of a slave-driver, happy to leave frieze work and matters of detailing to his draughtsmen. He might roughly sketch a particular pattern and then say, "Have a go at doing something like that." The draughtsman's work would immediately be accepted if it was up to standard. Westerholm left for Australia in 1936, but Louis Hay, the Natusch brothers, E A

Williams and Walter P Finch all stayed in Napier.

Although the sudden destruction of Napier provided the town with the clean slate so desired by the European *avant-garde,* especially Le Corbusier (1887-1966), the local architects preferred less adventurous solutions. Certainly Le Corbusier's notions, many of them in sharp opposition to those decorative principles illustrated at the 1925 Paris Exhibition of Decorative Arts, were known in New Zealand. A summary of his book *Towards a New Architecture* had appeared in the *NZIA Journal* in late 1929 but it was not until a decade later that the so-called International style had any impact at all in New Zealand.

In the thirties English architects were encouraged and influenced by the great Bauhaus figures, Marcel Breuer (1902-1981) and Walter Gropius (1883-1969) during their periods of residence in that country. Among those were New Zealanders, Amyas Connell of New Plymouth (1901-1980) and Basil Ward, (1902-1976) who had worked in Napier with Louis Hay from 1918 to 1920 and maintained a lifelong admiration of his work.

One building for a Mr Wilkinson, designed and built by W Atherfold in 1939, shows some evidence of familiarity with the cube-like unornamented solid forms favoured by these European architects. Its roofs and walls are flat, its windows flush with the wall surface and its Cathedral Lane location, next to the Ross and Glendinning building, allows immediate comparison with another plain but finely articulated Art Deco building.

As a result of the earthquake's upthrust, 3200 hectares of dry land had been created in place of the former marshy lagoon. Napier's new suburb of Marewa ("raised from the sea") was developed after 1935 following a lease agreement between the Borough Council and the Harbour Board, which still owned the new land.

It is in this area that most of the city's so-called Moderne houses are found. Indeed, Tom Parker Avenue and the streets around it offer an astonishing number of variations on the style. In most of them slightly inclined roofs are concealed behind a parapet which runs unbroken across the front and around the sides. Although the Moderne house has its weatherboard variant, walls are usually stuccoed and the absolute flatness is often relieved by horizontal bands above or below windows. Decorative plaster motifs appear at corners, on chimneys, and above entrances and windows, in an attempt to counter that plainness so vigorously promoted by Le Corbusier. Once again the sunburst, the zigzag, clouds and all sorts of geometric squiggles make an appearance.

The alternation of cube-like forms with "hat-box" curves is perhaps the best-

Napier Borough Council members and workmen gathered in 1933 to be photographed on completion of a bridge across the old bed of the Tutaekuri River, at the junction of George's Drive and Kennedy Road. The Kennedy Road extension thus formed opened up the suburb of Marewa. At left are E W Clement, Borough Surveyor and later Town Planner, and (in suit and hat) D Corbett, Borough Engineer.

known feature of these Moderne houses. Simple casement windows sweep around the exterior curved stucco walls giving a streamlined sense of spaciousness often contradicted by rather pokey interiors.

These houses without eaves encountered overheating problems and today many of them sport brightly coloured awnings in a variety of inappropriate materials. A similar problem also arose in the central business district, and even the magnificent simplicity of the Bank of New Zealand building was encased within an ugly metal-and-perspex verandah shield, recently removed in a major restoration of the building.

However, the happily temporary fate of this Napier Deco masterpiece was not as bad as that of the two-storeyed UFS Dispensary, built in 1932 to a modest Spanish-style design by Finch and Westerholm. This building, demolished as recently as 1986, was replaced by a structure mistakenly described as being "more Art Deco than the original", and is a crucial loss. Such destruction of heritage should not be repeated and it is worth noting by comparison the beneficial effect on the streetscape of the award-winning reconstruction of another pharmacy – Gahagan's – where the original facade was retained.

By January 1933 it was decided that the rebuilt city was ready to to be shown off to New Zealand. A crowded calendar of events was planned for the New Napier Week Carnival and the hardships of the Depression were briefly forgotten.

Once again the Governor-General and Lady Bledisloe came to Napier for the Grand Procession on 21 January. Two hundred and fifty decorated vehicles took part; Charles Kingsford-Smith flew over in his aircraft *Southern Cross;* the Napier Frivolity Minstrels, New Zealand's oldest performing arts group, played to thousands; a corrugated iron structure labelled "Ta-Ta Tin Town" clattered by.

A fortnight later the city's heads were bowed at a ceremony in memory of those who had died in the earthquake. A thanksgiving service was held at McLean Park where Commissioner Barton, described as "an amiable and gentle *Mussolini*" – words which at the time appeared quite complimentary – made one of his last speeches. The first meeting of the new Napier Borough Council was held on 15 May, 1933.

In the town, most buildings proudly proclaimed their newness through their date-bearing facades. Their architects, forswearing a post-colonialist return to English styles, had looked to the United States to give their city an authentically modern appearance. The range of stylistic borrowings they made in those difficult years made Napier architecturally unique. The City Beautiful, it was called in 1933 – and remains.

At the 1933 Napier Carnival the Portland Cement Company's float featured a model of Louis Hay's Central Fire Station.

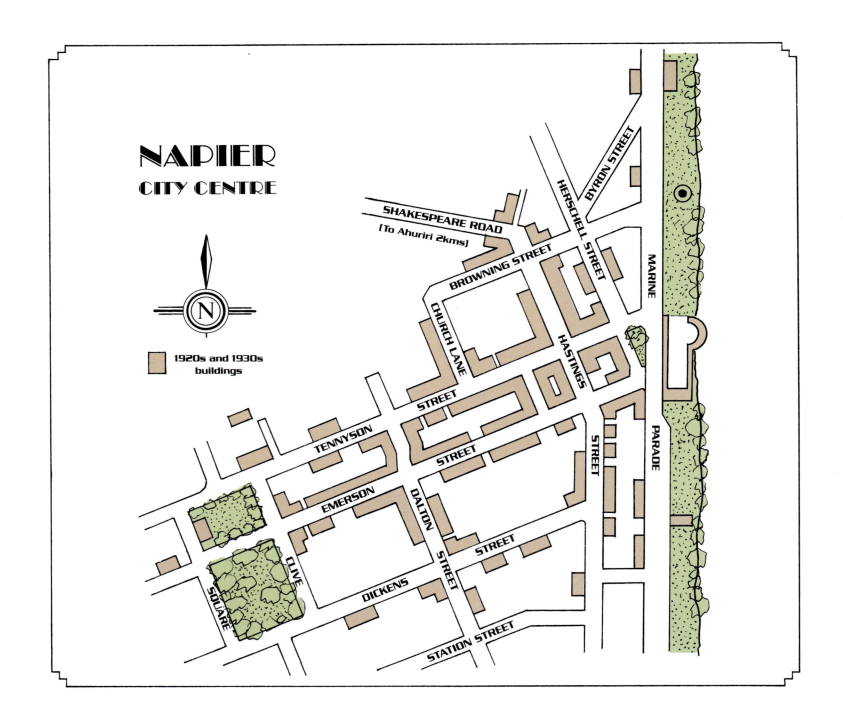

The Countrywide Bank Building on the Emerson Street - Dalton Street intersection. One of Napier's premier Art Deco buildings, it was originally designed by E A Williams in 1931 as the Hotel Central. The Countrywide Banking Corporation has carried out extensive restoration and redecoration of the exterior.

Left and top: Details of the Countrywide Bank Building's balconies, showing Art Deco zigzags and sunbursts symmetrically balanced on an almost flat facade.
Above: Leadlights on the stairwell.

The classic Art Deco sunburst is used as a design feature on stair railings, doors and windows throughout the building.
The ceiling lay-light of clear cut glass beneath a skylight was a popular solution to the problem of the dark interior.

Left: The Daily Telegraph Building, designed by
E A Williams in 1932.
The beautiful detailing throughout this building, both
inside and out, is typical of the period.

The Masonic Hotel, designed by W J Prouse of Wellington in 1932. Removal of a signboard above the Marine Parade entrance in 1988 revealed once more the original raised plaster lettering in a bold Art Deco style.

Above: Pergola verandahs, another Mediterranean feature, were very much in vogue in sunny climates like Napier's. The prevailing wind from the sea prevents the growth of climbing plants, and for this reason Louis Hay's proposed Albion Hotel to be sited further along the Parade was designed to face north.

Right: The Masonic Hotel is the only post-1931 building in Napier with ornamented pediments - too many people had been killed during the earthquake by falling masonry from such features.

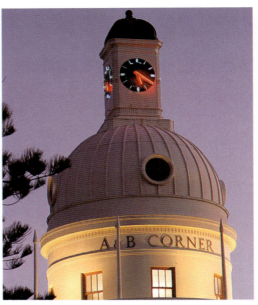

The A & B Building (formerly the T & G) was designed by Atkins & Mitchell in 1936 and is perhaps the city's most prominent landmark. At night the illuminated clock still shines out over Napier like the lighthouse from which its shape derives.

The former Ministry of Works Building also has its 'Lighthouse Tower' in the forecourt. It was designed by the Government Architect J T Mair in 1936.

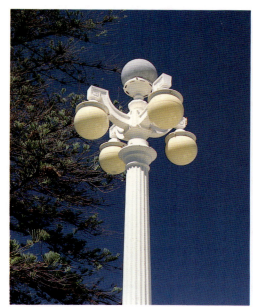

Top: The Marine Parade lamps are of a style found in other New Zealand towns, including nearby Hastings.

Above: The Sun Bay sits on rubble from buildings demolished after the earthquake.

Left: The New Napier Arch on the Marine Parade was designed by J T Watson, Napier Borough Council Architect.

Right: The Tom Parker Fountain in the Marine Parade Gardens is closely modelled on one in Bournemouth, England.

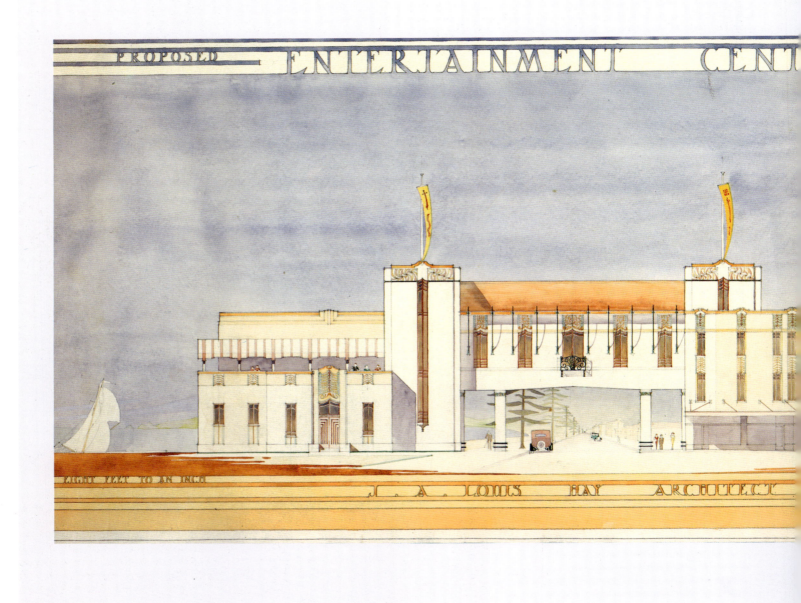

PROPOSED ENTERTAINMENT CEN...

EIGHT FEET TO AN INCH

J. A. LOUIS HAY ARCHITECT

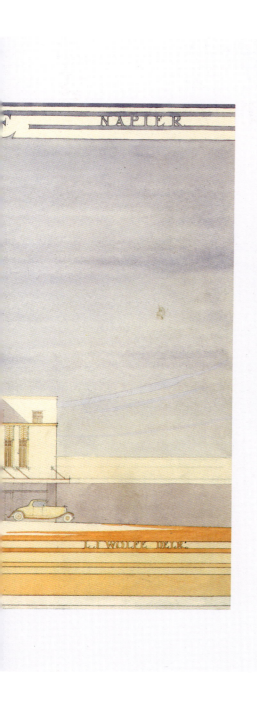

Left: Louis Hay's ambitious Entertainment Centre spanning the Marine Parade was never built. Although large drawings of this scheme were prominently displayed for the citizens of Napier to admire, money was short and the project abandoned. This watercolour rendering is by Leonard Wolfe, who worked in Hay's office in 1933 and 1934.

Above: J T Watson's more modest Soundshell was built on the site originally intended for the Entertainment Centre. The photograph also shows part of the formal Marine Parade Gardens between the Soundshell and the Tom Parker Fountain. Immediately in front of the Soundshell is the original Napier Outdoor Skating Rink - a concrete area facing the Sun Bay which is edged by an Art Deco zigzag pattern inlaid in coloured concrete.

Left: Masson House, designed by
E A Williams in 1931 and *(below)* Louis Hay's
unusually restrained Hildebrandt Building of
1932, designed for a client who specified the
decorative use of an undulating wave motif
linking the German and New Zealand flags.
Above: The Salmon Motors Building and the
elegant little office building at Ahuriri were
designed by unknown architects.

The Kidson's Corner Building, originally the Smith & Chambers Building, was designed by H Alfred Hill of Napier in 1932. It exhibits a number of classic Art Deco features, as does the medallion above the ABH Building nearby in Emerson Street.

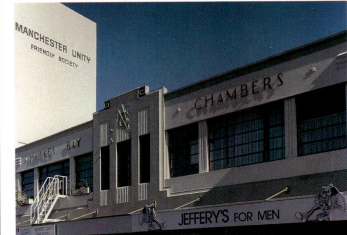

Left & Top: Hawke's Bay Chambers - architect unknown - has a striking central feature and fine interior wood panelling.
Below: On this Emerson Street building, also by an unknown architect, redecoration has enhanced the Art Deco detailing.

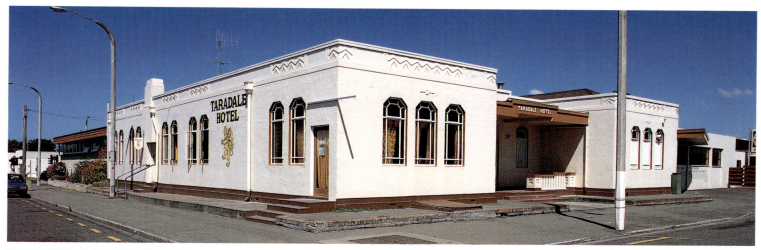

In the 1930s Taradale was a Borough in its own right, but it is now an outlying suburb of Napier. The Taradale Hotel and Town Hall are its major Art Deco buildings. The stained glass window in the Town Hall was installed in place of the original entrance doors in a recent reconstruction. Also shown is the Napier Gospel Hall, near Clive Square.

The ASB Bank, restored and refurbished in 1993, was originally
built in 1932 as premises for the Bank of New Zealand. The
design, by the Wellington partnership Crichton, McKay &
Haughton, makes great use of Maori motifs.

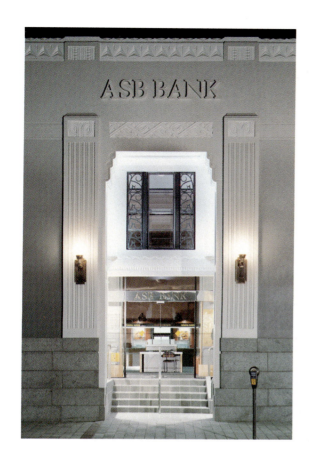

Above: On the lintel over the main entrance the similarity between the Art Deco zigzag and a *kowhaiwhai* pattern has been exploited.
A borrowed Maori carving motif tops the pilasters in the richly decorated interior. Another *kowhaiwhai* pattern adorns the panels surrounding the coffered skylights and the mask of a *taiaha* looks down from the corners.

This building in Cathedral Lane was designed as premises for Ross & Glendinning by E A Williams in 1932. Its simple facade is subtly decorated with an adaptation of a Maori rafter pattern based on the *pitau* or fern frond.

PUBLIC TRUST OFFICE

The neo-classical Public Trust Building not only withstood the earthquake, but also escaped the fire which swept through the city immediately afterwards. It was designed by Eric Phillips of Hastings.

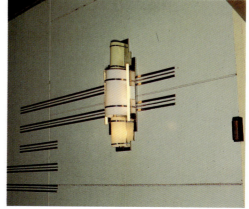

The Municipal Theatre, built in 1937 to the design of J T Watson, the Borough Architect. The original prize-winning design by Louis Hay was rejected as being too expensive, yet the completed structure has many elaborate Art Deco features.

Legal Offices designed by Finch & Westerholm for Sainsbury,
Logan & Williams in 1931.

Napier has a number of leadlight glass domes, among them *(above)* one over the entrance foyer of Sainsbury, Logan & Williams, and another which bears a very strong resemblance to it *(right)* in the former Trocadero Tearooms, later known as the Napier Cafe.

Left: Halsbury Chambers in Tennyson Street is the work of an unknown architect.

Below: The Market Reserve Building designed by the Associated Architects out of the office of Natusch & Sons was the first to be completed after the earthquake - it boasts bronze metal windows and panels which were supplied by their British manufacturer at the price of steel ones as a gesture to the devastated city.

The foundation stone of Louis Hay's distinctively Californian 'Women's Rest' in Clive Square was laid by Sir Charles Fergusson in 1925. The building was destroyed in the earthquake, but rebuilt in 1934.

Louis Hay's home for Miss Doris Dolbel dates from 1918. The leadlights in the hall, although deceptively Art Deco in appearance, show the influence of Frank Lloyd Wright's window designs for his 1903 Dana house in Springfield, Illinois.

The hanging ceiling light looks remarkably similar to those designed by Californian architects Charles and Henry Greene in the first decade of this century.

Louis Hay designed 'Mornington' in 1921, incorporating many features of the Californian bungalow appropriate to Napier's sunny climate.

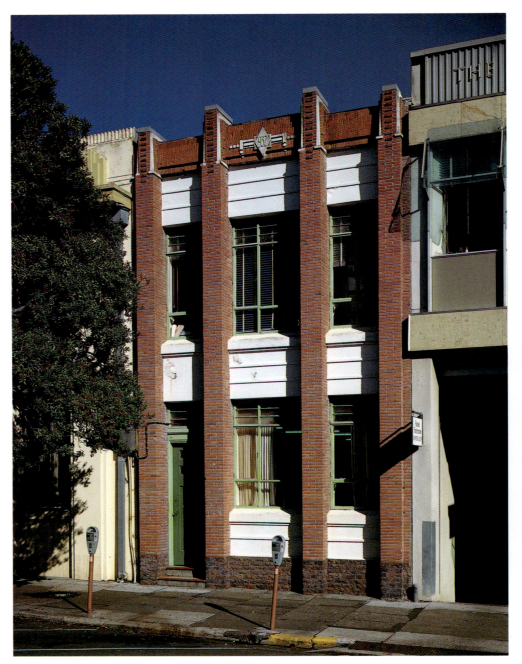

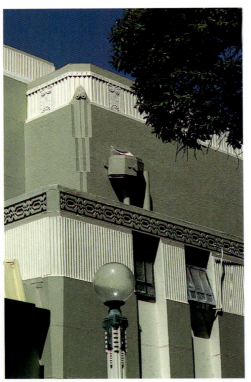

Left: Hay's own offices in Herschell Street, built in 1932 to replace his earthquake-damaged premises.

Left: A glimpse of some fine detailing on the Napier Art Gallery, designed by Louis Hay in 1935.
Above & Right: Fine detailing is also evident in both exterior and interior doors of the building.

In 1930 Louis Hay designed these windows for the home of Gerhard Husheer, owner of the National Tobacco Company. The leadlights are testimony to the skill of Douglas Pirie, who began work with Hay in 1926. The unusual hall screen is closely modelled on a door design by the Italian architect Raimondo D'Aronco (1857-1932) for the Administration Building of the 1902 Turin Exhibition of Modern Decorative Arts.

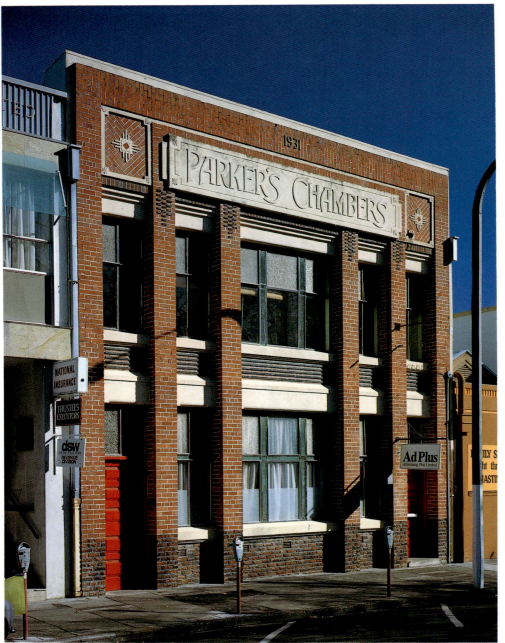

Left: Louis Hay designed a new brick facade on Herschell Street for Parker's Chambers in 1930. When this collapsed he replaced it with another.

Above: The contrasting Hastings Street entrance was built in 1932. All verandahs had to be suspended rather than held up by posts, so Hay fancifully designed metal supporting rods held in the mouths of lions.

Right: The Self Help Shoppers Fair, designed by Louis Hay in 1932, and Hayne's Building, a butcher's premises, built in the same year.
Below: Abbott's Building owes much of its decoration, as well as its long horizontal central window line, to the influence of Frank Lloyd Wright, particularly his Robie House, Chicago, of 1909. It was designed by Louis Hay and J B Frame.

The 1933 AMP Building, now the legal offices of Callinicos
Gallagher, in which Louis Hay used elaborate floral motifs similar
to those used by the great Chicago architect Louis Sullivan.

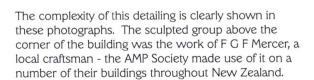

The complexity of this detailing is clearly shown in these photographs. The sculpted group above the corner of the building was the work of F G F Mercer, a local craftsman - the AMP Society made use of it on a number of their buildings throughout New Zealand.

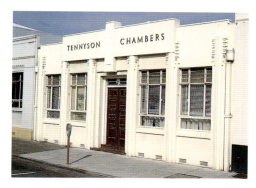

Plans for the Munster and Tennyson Chambers originated in the offices of C T Natusch & Sons, but exterior detailing is unmistakably the work of Louis Hay's office. On Tennyson Chambers the influence of Frank Lloyd Wright's geometric designs is apparent, while Munster Chambers - named after an Irish County and originally painted green - features clusters of shamrocks.

Left: Interior details of the AMP Building after restoration in 1993. The staircase had been repositioned in earlier alterations, but is now restored to its original position within the alcove designed for it. The elaborate detailing of the interior doors and light fittings and the plaster work in the reception area are all typical Louis Hay designs.

Left: The Desco Building was originally designed in red brick as the Napier Fire Station in 1921. Louis Hay reconditioned it in 1931, adding adjoining accommodation for Fire Officers *(right)*.

Hay frequently made use of decorative concrete pendants such as these on the Desco Building and on the sadly neglected Ellison and Duncan Building *(above)*.

The Rothman's Building, originally designed by Louis Hay for the National Tobacco Company in 1933. Here, no expense was spared.

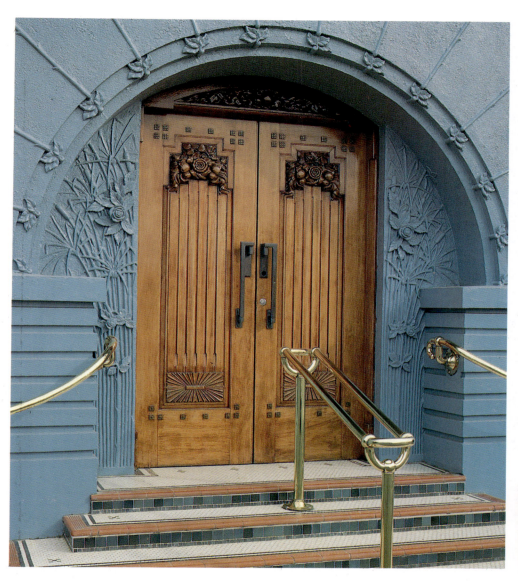

The arched entrance was a device much used by Sullivan and Wright as well as by contemporary English and Austrian architects. Hay exuberantly used a combination of sculpted concrete raupo and roses, sunbursts and bunches of fruit, in conjunction with polished wood, gleaming brass and mosaic tiles.

Inside the Rothman's Building the decorative scheme is enriched by polished marble and a domed skylight. The stained glass leaded lights above the counter are a much later addition - their modern construction jars alongside the original workmanship.

The Spanish style, with twisted columns, laid 'cordova' roof tiles and curved parapets, was chosen by architects Finch & Westerholm for the Provincial Hotel in 1932. There is an unusual leadlight designed around an arrangement of wine glasses above a side entrance and the original plaster ceiling has been restored in the corner bar.

The Crown Hotel in Ahuriri is the work of an unknown architect.
It too displays some Spanish influence.

74

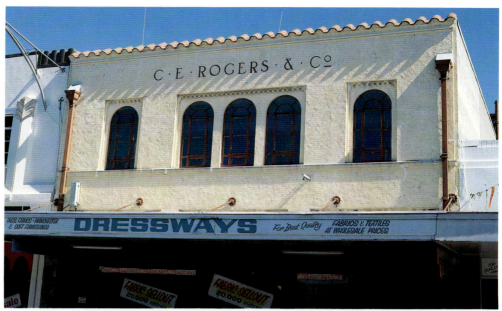

Above: The balcony of Holland's Building was designed by Arthur Marshall, a young Auckland architecture graduate who worked with E A Williams in the early thirties.
Above right: C E Rogers & Co's building, designed by Finch & Westerholm in 1932.
Right: The Emerson Building, named after the street in which it is situated, is by an unknown architect.

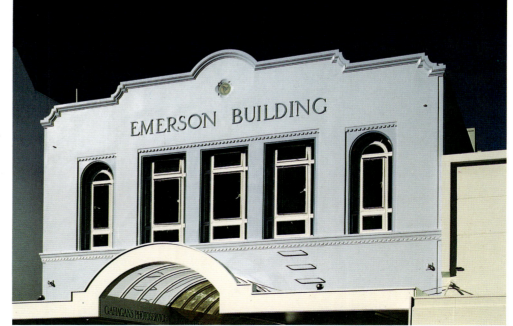

Finch & Westerholm also designed the State Cinema *(left)* of 1933, again in Spanish style. Unfortunately their 1931 UFS Dispensary Building *(top)* was demolished in 1986. *(Above)* The distinctly Art Deco window combining Napier's Marine Parade Norfolk Island pines, the sky and the sea is above the staircase of the Criterion Hotel.

Designed by E A Williams in 1932, the Criterion Hotel has a Spanish facade. A recent major fire destroyed the floor and roof of the building, but the structure was fortunately so robust that a complete restoration proved possible.

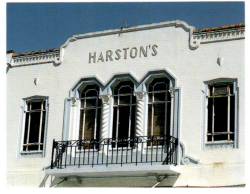

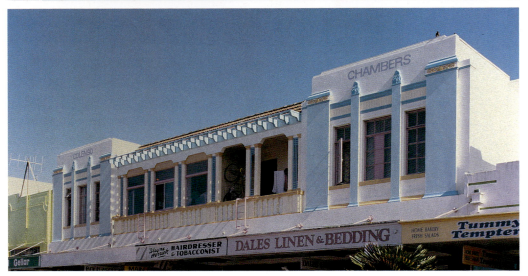

Top left: The former Gaiety de Luxe Cinema, built in 1932 - it is perhaps the most 'Spanish' of all Napier's buildings.

Bottom left: Colenso Chambers was originally designed as the County Hotel in Emerson Street.

Above: Harston's Building, designed in the Spanish style by E A Williams in 1930. Although badly shaken in the earthquake, the structure was successfully 'caged' in 1931 and the Spanish facade preserved.

Right: Harston's Music Shop as it was known to Napier residents for sixty years - although the refined detailing of the shop front was not affected in its recent conversion to a restaurant, much of the glass has been rendered opaque.

THACKERAY HOUSE

This attractive building dating from the Victorian era was remodelled in the Moderne style in 1934. It was regrettably demolished in spite of intense public protest, to make way for a supermarket of uncompromising architectural sterility.

Left: This well-proportioned Modernist building was designed as a music studio and built by W Atherfold of Napier in Cathedral Lane in 1939.

The popular Moderne style on a large scale - Ranui Flats on the Marine Parade.

Following the shifting of land in the earthquake, large areas to the south of Napier became available for housing and the new suburb of Marewa was opened up in 1933. Many of Napier's best examples of the Moderne style are to be found in this vicinity.

The Hawke's Bay Harbour Board Building was designed by
William, Williams, Davies & Phillip of Napier and built in 1940.

INDEX

GLOSSARY

Adobe   unfired, sun-dried brick, commonly used for building in Spain, Latin America and Western USA. The adobe look was popular for Spanish Mission buildings, which were often plastered and painted white.

Bas-relief   sculpted figures or patterns which do not stand far out from the surface on which they are formed.

Bay   a vertical division in the exterior of a building, marked by an arrangement of windows, pillars or roofing.

Campanario   a bell tower, a popular feature in the Spanish Mission style.

Capital   the head or crown of a column.

Casement window   a window with the opening frame hung vertically, opening outwards or inwards. (By comparison, in a sash window, the frame slides vertically in grooves.)

Chevron   a moulding which forms a zigzag shape.

Coffering   a ceiling decoration consisting of sunken squares.

Cornice   a projecting ornamental moulding along the top of a wall or arch.

Eaves   the underpart of a sloping roof overhanging a wall or verandah.

Espadana   a curved parapet at the top of a shaped gable.

Facing   the finish applied to the outer surface of a building.

Gable   the triangular upper portion of a wall at the end of a pitched roof.

Lintel   a horizontal beam or stone which bridges an opening.

Mosaic   surface decoration for walls, floors or steps formed of small pieces of glass, stone or marble.

Parapet   a low wall placed at the top of a house.

Pediment   the triangular (or segmental) upright front end of a moderately-pitched roof.

Pergola   a covered verandah made of wood or stone posts or pillars with open joists above, sometimes covered with climbing plants.

Pilaster   a shallow rectangular column projecting only slightly from a wall.

Scotia   a concave moulding.

Stucco   plaster work, often with a textured pattern.

The Cosmos Collection